Quilt as You Go

Create Stunning Quilts One Block at a Time

CW01507815

Collins Palmer
copyright@2024

Table of Content

CHAPTER ONE
Getting Started with Quilt as You Go (QAYG)

Quilt as You Go (QAYG) is a quilting technique that allows quilters to piece and quilt their projects simultaneously. Unlike traditional quilting, where the entire quilt top is assembled before quilting, QAYG enables you to work on individual blocks or sections, quilting them as you go. This method not only simplifies the process but also makes handling larger quilts more manageable since you work with smaller, more manageable pieces.

QAYG is ideal for both beginners and experienced quilters looking for a quick and efficient way to complete projects. It offers flexibility in design, allowing you to experiment with different patterns, fabrics, and layouts. By quilting each block or section individually, you have more control over the quilting process, resulting in a polished and professional-looking quilt with minimal bulk.

This technique is perfect for quilters who may not have access to large quilting spaces or long-arm machines, as it reduces the complexity of quilting large pieces of fabric. Whether you're creating small projects like table runners or larger quilts, QAYG makes quilting enjoyable, efficient, and less overwhelming.

Benefits of Quilt as You Go (QAYG)

Manageability: QAYG allows you to work with smaller sections of your quilt at a time, making the process easier to handle. This is especially helpful for larger quilts, where managing the entire quilt top and layers can be bulky and challenging.

Faster Completion: By piecing and quilting simultaneously, you save time in the overall process. Once your blocks or sections are quilted, the quilt is almost finished, reducing the need for additional quilting after assembling the top.

Precision Quilting: With QAYG, each block or section is quilted individually, giving you more control over the quilting process. This results in more precise stitches and better overall quality.

Less Bulk: Traditional quilting requires working with large fabric pieces, which can be cumbersome. QAYG eliminates this issue by breaking the project into smaller, more manageable sections that are easier to maneuver.

Creative Flexibility: Since QAYG allows you to quilt block by block, you can experiment with different designs, fabrics, or quilting techniques within each section. This method is perfect for those who want to add variety and creativity to their quilts.

Beginner-Friendly: For beginners, QAYG is an approachable technique. You don't need a large space or advanced quilting skills to get started. It provides a gradual introduction to quilting while building skills block by block.

Budget-Friendly: Because QAYG requires fewer materials upfront (you can use scraps or smaller batting pieces), it's cost-effective. You also don't need access to large quilting machines or spaces, saving money on equipment.

Easier for Domestic Sewing Machines: Since you work with smaller sections, domestic sewing machines can handle the quilting process without difficulty, making it accessible to more quilters.

Portable: QAYG allows you to take small sections of your project with you, making it easier to quilt on the go. This is great for quilters who enjoy working on their projects while traveling or at quilting meet-ups.

Quilt-as-You-Go Variety: You can choose from various QAYG techniques—whether it's joining quilted blocks with sashing or using join-as-you-go methods—which gives you flexibility in how you assemble your quilt.

Understanding the Quilt as You Go (QAYG) Technique

The Quilt as You Go (QAYG) technique simplifies the quilting process by combining piecing and quilting into one step. Instead of constructing the entire quilt top first and then quilting it as a whole, you quilt each block or section individually and then join them together. This method reduces the complexity of managing large quilt tops and allows for more control and creativity over each block.

Key Components of QAYG

Individual Quilted Blocks or Sections: In QAYG, you quilt smaller sections, typically one block at a time. Each block includes the quilt top, batting, and backing, and you can complete the quilting before moving on to the next block. This makes the process less daunting, especially for larger quilts.

Layering: Each block or section is layered with the fabric for the top, batting, and backing fabric—just like you would with a full quilt. The main difference is that you're working on much smaller pieces. This layering is essential to ensure that every block is fully quilted.

Quilting Each Block: After layering, you quilt the block as desired. Since you're working on a small section, you have more control over your stitching and can easily execute detailed designs. Whether you're doing straight-line quilting, free-motion quilting, or decorative stitching, the smaller surface area is easier to work with.

Joining the Blocks: Once you have quilted your individual blocks, the next step is joining them together. The most common method is to add strips of fabric called sashing to connect the blocks. These sashing strips can be used to hide the seams and give the quilt a cohesive look. Some QAYG techniques allow you to join blocks without sashing by using a join-as-you-go approach, which involves attaching quilted blocks directly to one another.

Finishing the Quilt: Once all the blocks are joined, you'll need to add borders (if desired), then finish the quilt with binding around the edges, just like a traditional quilt. The result is a fully quilted piece without the bulk and complexity of handling a large quilt top all at once.

QAYG Variations

There are several variations of the QAYG technique, each with its unique approach:

Traditional QAYG: Each block is quilted individually, and sashing strips are used to join them together.

Join-As-You-Go: This method connects blocks without adding sashing, using seam allowances or other techniques to join pre-quilted sections.

Block-by-Block QAYG: Each block is quilted and bound individually before being connected to form the final quilt.

Advantages of Understanding QAYG

Learning how to manage the individual blocks and sections before assembly gives you more creative freedom. You can customize the quilting for each section, use up fabric scraps, and even experiment with different quilting styles or designs across the quilt. Additionally, QAYG allows you to see progress as you go, offering a satisfying sense of accomplishment with each block completed.

This technique also makes quilting accessible to beginners and more advanced quilters alike, as it simplifies the physical work of quilting and breaks it down into manageable steps.

Choosing Fabrics and Batting for Quilt as You Go (QAYG)

Selecting the right fabrics and batting is crucial for creating a successful Quilt as You Go (QAYG) project. Since each block is quilted individually, the materials you choose will affect the overall look, feel, and durability of the quilt. Here's a guide to help you make the best choices.

Fabrics for QAYG

Quilting Cotton: Quilting cotton is the most common choice for both the top and back of your quilt. It's durable, easy to work with, and comes in a variety of colors and patterns. The tight weave makes it ideal for quilting, as it holds stitches well and doesn't fray easily.

Scraps and Precuts: QAYG is perfect for using up fabric scraps or precut fabric like fat quarters, jelly rolls, or charm packs. Since you're working with individual blocks, small pieces of fabric can be combined in creative ways, giving your quilt a unique, scrappy look.

Consideration for Backing Fabric: The backing fabric for each block will be visible from the back of the quilt, so consider how it complements your top fabrics. You can choose to use the same fabric for all block backings for a cohesive look, or mix it up for a more eclectic style.

Solid fabrics for backing create a clean, unified look.

Patterns or prints can add visual interest, especially for reversible quilts.

Color and Pattern Selection

Color Coordination: Choose fabrics that complement each other across the quilt. You can go for a monochromatic theme, complementary colors, or a bold contrast.

Pattern Balance: If you're using bold prints on the top, consider using solids or simple patterns on the back to balance the design.

If the blocks are simple, feel free to experiment with patterned backing fabrics.

Fabric Quality: High-quality quilting fabrics will last longer and hold up well through frequent handling and washing. Look for fabrics that are 100% cotton with a tight weave to avoid fraying and distortion over time.

Batting for QAYG

The type of batting you use is just as important as the fabrics in creating a quilt that feels soft, warm, and well-constructed. Since you'll be working with smaller sections, you can use leftover batting scraps or purchase new batting, depending on your project.

Cotton Batting: Cotton batting is popular for its soft texture and breathability. It has a low loft (thin thickness), which makes it ideal for QAYG since it doesn't add too much bulk to each individual block. It's easy to work with and holds up well after multiple washes, making it a durable option.

Polyester Batting: Polyester batting is known for its higher loft, which gives quilts a fluffier, more textured look. While it adds more volume, it's lightweight and often less expensive than cotton. However, it can shift more easily, so it's important to secure the layers well during quilting.

Cotton-Poly Blend: A cotton-poly blend combines the benefits of both cotton and polyester. It has the softness and durability of cotton with a bit more loft from the polyester. This option provides a balance between a flat and fluffy appearance, and it's often easier to quilt through than pure polyester.

Wool Batting: Wool batting is warm, lightweight, and has a higher loft, which can add extra texture to your quilt. It's ideal for colder climates but may require more care in washing, as wool can shrink or felt if handled improperly.

Batting Scraps: Since QAYG allows for quilting in smaller sections, you can use up batting scraps from previous projects. Just make sure to join them securely, either by overlapping slightly or by zigzag stitching to prevent gaps.

Batting Thickness (Loft)

Low Loft: If you prefer a thinner, more traditional-looking quilt, low-loft batting is the way to go. It's easier to work with, especially for beginners, and adds minimal bulk to each block.

High Loft: For a puffier, more textured look, high-loft batting adds extra depth and dimension. However, it requires more attention when quilting to prevent bunching or shifting.

Considerations for QAYG Projects

Handling and Quilting: Since QAYG involves quilting smaller blocks, it's easier to work with different types of fabrics and batting. However, when combining different fabric types or batting thicknesses, make sure to test your machine's tension and stitch length to avoid uneven quilting.

Fabric and Batting Shrinkage: Both fabric and batting can shrink when washed. Pre-wash your fabrics to prevent shrinking later, and if you're using cotton batting, consider pre-washing it as well. This helps ensure that your quilt doesn't warp after it's been washed for the first time.

Mixing and Matching: QAYG encourages creativity, so don't hesitate to mix different fabrics and batting types for different blocks. This adds variety and texture to your quilt, making each section unique.

Essential Tools and Materials Needed

To successfully complete a Quilt as You Go (QAYG) project, having the right tools and materials is crucial. Below is a list of the essentials you will need to get started.

Fabric

Quilting cotton: Choose high-quality quilting cotton for your quilt top. This fabric is durable, easy to sew, and comes in a wide variety of colors and patterns.

Backing Fabric: You'll need fabric for the back of each block or the entire quilt. Make sure it complements the front design.

Binding Fabric: For finishing your quilt, you'll need strips of fabric to bind the edges.

Batting

Batting is the layer that adds warmth and thickness to your quilt. Options include:

Cotton Batting: Ideal for a traditional look and feel.

Polyester Batting: Provides a fluffier finish and is lighter in weight.

Wool Batting: Offers extra warmth and loft, though it's more expensive.

For QAYG, consider cutting your batting slightly smaller than your fabric to reduce bulk in the seams.

Sewing Machine

A basic sewing machine with straight stitching capabilities works well for QAYG. However, a machine with quilting features (e.g., adjustable stitch length, quilting foot options) can make the process smoother.

Walking Foot: This is highly recommended for even feeding of fabric layers through the machine.

Free-motion quilting foot (optional): Ideal for more intricate quilting designs.

Rotary Cutter, Cutting Mat, and Ruler

Rotary cutter: A sharp rotary cutter ensures clean, straight cuts for your fabric and batting.

Cutting mat: A self-healing cutting mat protects your work surface and helps keep your cuts precise.

Quilting ruler: Use a clear acrylic ruler for accurate measurements when cutting blocks, strips, and binding.

Thread

Use high-quality cotton or polyester thread. Ensure the color blends or contrasts well with your fabric, depending on your desired look. You may need different colors for quilting and piecing.

Quilting Needles

For machine quilting, use quilting needles that can handle the thickness of your layers. A size 90/14 needle is often ideal for quilting cotton fabric and batting.

For hand quilting, opt for needles specifically designed for quilting, such as "betweens."

Pins or Clips

Quilting pins: Long, sturdy pins help hold layers in place while you sew.

Clips: Fabric clips can be a great alternative to pins, especially for binding or when dealing with thicker seams.

Fabric Marking Tools

Use fabric-safe pens or chalk to mark your quilting lines, seams, or cutting guidelines. These markings should be removable, so choose tools that disappear with water or heat.

Iron and Pressing Surface

Pressing is a key step in QAYG, so a good iron is essential. A steam iron works best to flatten seams and blocks as you go.

A heat-resistant pressing mat or ironing board provides a smooth surface for pressing your quilt.

Basting Spray or Pins

For securing your fabric, batting, and backing layers before quilting:

Basting spray: A temporary adhesive spray holds the layers together without shifting.

Basting pins: Curved safety pins are useful for keeping the layers secure.

Measuring Tape

Keep a measuring tape handy to check dimensions, especially when arranging blocks and ensuring uniform size.

Quilting Gloves (optional)

Quilting gloves offer extra grip and control when feeding your quilt sandwich through the machine. This is particularly useful for larger projects.

Seam Ripper

Mistakes happen, and a seam ripper allows you to carefully undo stitches without damaging the fabric.

CHAPTER TWO
Preparing Your Blocks

Cutting Fabric for Quilt as You Go (QAYG) Blocks

Accurately cutting fabric for QAYG blocks is crucial for ensuring your quilt pieces align properly and fit together seamlessly. Since each block will be pieced and quilted individually, having the right measurements and clean cuts will make the assembly process easier and more precise.

Tools for Cutting Fabric

Rotary Cutter: A rotary cutter is the most efficient tool for cutting fabric for quilting. It ensures smooth, clean edges and allows for precise cuts, especially when paired with a cutting mat and ruler. Opt for a 45mm rotary cutter for most projects, and consider a smaller 28mm cutter for intricate cuts or smaller pieces.

Self-Healing Cutting Mat: A self-healing cutting mat protects your work surface and allows for smooth, clean cuts with your rotary cutter. Make sure the mat is large enough to accommodate the fabric pieces you're cutting. Gridlines on the mat can help with measuring and aligning your fabric.

Acrylic Ruler: An acrylic quilting ruler is essential for measuring and cutting straight lines. Look for a ruler with clear, easy-to-read markings and a non-slip feature to prevent shifting while cutting. The most common size is 6" x 24", but smaller rulers can be useful for trimming small blocks.

Fabric Scissors: While a rotary cutter is ideal for precision cutting, fabric scissors are handy for cutting small pieces of fabric, threads, or curves that may not be suitable for a rotary cutter.

Marking Tools: Use fabric-safe marking tools such as chalk pencils, disappearing ink pens, or water-soluble markers to mark cutting lines on your fabric, especially for intricate cuts or patterns.

Steps for Cutting Fabric for QAYG Blocks

Prepare and Press the Fabric: Before cutting, press your fabric to remove any wrinkles or creases. This ensures that your measurements are accurate and that the fabric lays flat, making cutting easier.

Measure the Blocks: Decide on the size of your QAYG blocks. Common sizes include 6", 8", or 12" squares, but you can choose any size based on your project needs. Remember that each block will include a seam allowance, so add ¼" to each side of the block for seams. For example, if you want a 6" finished block, cut the fabric to 6 ½" to account for seam allowances.

Layering for Multiple Cuts: To save time, you can layer multiple pieces of fabric and cut them simultaneously. Stack the fabrics neatly, ensuring that the edges align, then cut through the layers with your rotary cutter. Just make sure your rotary cutter blade is sharp to avoid jagged edges.

Aligning the Fabric: Place your fabric on the cutting mat, making sure it is smooth and flat. Align the edges of your fabric with the gridlines on your cutting mat to ensure that your cuts are straight and even.

Cutting the Blocks: Use the acrylic ruler to measure and align your cut lines. Place the ruler over the fabric, ensuring it is square with the fabric edges and cutting mat lines. Hold the ruler firmly with one hand, and use the rotary cutter to slice along the ruler's edge. Keep your hand steady to prevent shifting and ensure an even cut.

Trimming the Edges: If your fabric edges are uneven or have been pre-cut but not straight, trim the edges before cutting your blocks. Align the fabric on the cutting mat, place the acrylic ruler along the edge, and trim off any uneven fabric with the rotary cutter.

Cutting Multiple Sizes or Shapes: Depending on your QAYG design, you may need blocks in various sizes or shapes (like triangles or strips). Measure each shape carefully and cut them with the rotary cutter, following the same process of aligning and cutting for clean, accurate pieces.

Tips for Cutting Fabric for QAYG Blocks

Test Cut: If you're working with new fabric or testing a new block size, make a test cut on a scrap piece of fabric to ensure accuracy before cutting all your blocks.

Use Sharp Blades: A sharp rotary cutter blade is essential for clean cuts. Dull blades can cause the fabric to fray or result in uneven cuts.

Stay Consistent: Consistency is key when cutting blocks for QAYG. Make sure all your blocks are cut to the same size so they fit together neatly during the assembly process.

Cut with Precision: Take your time to measure and cut with precision. Even small inaccuracies can lead to alignment issues when piecing and quilting the blocks together.

Tips for Piecing Blocks Together in Quilt as You Go (QAYG)

Piecing blocks together is a crucial step in the Quilt as You Go (QAYG) method, as it involves joining individually quilted sections into a cohesive quilt. Unlike traditional quilting, where the top is pieced and quilted as a whole, QAYG requires special attention to ensure that the pre-quilted blocks are connected neatly and securely.

Use Sashing for a Clean Look

Sashing is a popular method for joining QAYG blocks. It involves sewing strips of fabric between the quilted blocks, which helps to hide the seams and create a clean, polished look.

Cutting the Sashing Strips: Cut the sashing strips slightly wider than the seams of your blocks. For example, if your blocks have a ¼" seam allowance, cut the sashing strips ½" or ¾" wide to allow for easy folding and stitching.

Attaching Sashing: Sew one sashing strip to the edge of one block, right sides together. Press the seam open, then sew the adjoining block to the other side of the sashing strip. Repeat this process for all the blocks.

Wide or Narrow Sashing: You can experiment with different sashing widths depending on the design you want. Wider sashing gives a more modern, open look, while narrow sashing creates a tighter, more intricate pattern.

Match Seams for Precise Alignment

Accurate seam matching ensures that your blocks align perfectly, creating a professional-looking quilt.

Pin Seams: Before sewing, use pins to match the seams of adjoining blocks. Place a pin directly through the seams of both blocks and pin them together. This helps to keep the seams aligned as you sew.

Nesting Seams: If you're using sashing or joining two blocks without sashing, you can nest the seams by pressing one seam allowance to the left and the other to the right. This reduces bulk and ensures the seams lie flat against each other.

Trim Blocks Before Joining

Even with careful cutting and piecing, some blocks may end up slightly uneven. It's important to trim your blocks to ensure that all of them are the same size before piecing them together.

Use a Square Ruler: A square acrylic ruler is ideal for trimming blocks. Align the ruler with the block and trim away any excess fabric to ensure all blocks are uniform in size.

Check for Consistency: Double-check that all your blocks are the same size before moving forward with piecing. This consistency will help the quilt come together neatly.

Seam Allowances Matter

Since you are joining quilted blocks with their batting and backing in place, handling the seam allowances properly is crucial for a smooth finish.

Use a Consistent Seam Allowance: Stick to the same seam allowance throughout your project, typically ¼". This ensures that your blocks fit together correctly and that the quilt remains evenly sized.

Press Seams Open or to the Side: Pressing seams open or to the side can reduce bulk at the intersections of the blocks. Open seams lie flatter, while side-pressed seams add durability. Choose the option that best suits your project.

Consider a Quilt-as-You-Go Join Method

There are multiple ways to join quilted blocks without using sashing. These methods result in a cleaner, more traditional look where the blocks seem to be directly joined.

Butted Seams: To use butted seams, trim the batting from the seam allowance on both blocks and stitch the blocks together without additional batting. The seams will butt up against each other, creating a smooth join.

Zigzag or Ladder Stitch: Some quilters prefer to use a zigzag stitch or ladder stitch to join blocks directly by hand. This technique works especially well for joining blocks without adding extra fabric between them.

Test Your Machine Tension and Needle Size

Since you are sewing through multiple layers (the quilt top, batting, and backing), make sure your sewing machine is properly set up.

Adjust Tension: Test your machine tension on scrap fabric pieces with similar layers. Adjust the tension if necessary to prevent puckering or loose stitches.

Use a Strong Needle: A size 90/14 or 100/16 needle works well for piecing QAYG blocks together, as it can handle the thickness of the quilt layers.

Press Seams and Blocks After Joining

Pressing your seams and blocks after joining is an important step to achieving a flat, polished look.

Press Seams Flat: After sewing the blocks together, press the seams flat to reduce bulk. You can press the seams open or to one side depending on your preference.

Press the Entire Block: Once your seams are pressed, take a moment to press the entire block. This helps to smooth out any wrinkles and ensures that the joined blocks lie flat before you move on to the next step.

Be Mindful of Quilting Design Continuity

If you've created intricate quilting designs on your individual blocks, pay attention to how those designs connect once the blocks are joined.

Align Quilting Patterns: If you're using geometric or straight-line quilting, try to align the quilting lines between adjoining blocks for a continuous, cohesive look.

Filling in Gaps: Sometimes, small gaps or spaces between quilted sections may appear after joining. You can fill these in with additional quilting stitches to create a seamless finish.

Add Borders for a Finished Look

Adding borders around your quilt can give it a finished, professional look while also helping to stabilize the edges.

Wide or Narrow Borders: Choose the width of your borders based on your design preferences. Wider borders can add a striking frame, while narrow borders give a subtler finish.

Use Coordinating Fabrics: Choose fabrics for the borders that complement the colors and patterns in your quilt. Solid fabrics are often a good choice for borders, as they provide a clean finish without overwhelming the overall design.

Pressing Techniques for Best Results in Quilt as You Go (QAYG)

Pressing is an essential step in quilting that helps to flatten seams, ensure precision in piecing, and give your quilt a polished finish. Proper pressing techniques will make the Quilt as You Go (QAYG) process smoother, especially since you're working with individual quilted blocks. Here are some pressing techniques to achieve the best results.

Press, Don't Iron

One of the most important things to remember is to press rather than iron. Pressing involves lifting and setting the iron down onto the fabric, while ironing involves dragging the iron across the fabric.

Why Pressing Is Important: Pressing helps flatten seams without distorting the fabric, while ironing can stretch or warp the fabric, which may lead to misaligned blocks.

How to Press: Lift the iron and gently press it down on the area you want to flatten. Hold it in place for a few seconds, then lift it again before moving to the next spot.

Press Seams to the Side or Open

When piecing your QAYG blocks together, you'll need to decide whether to press your seams open or to the side. Both methods have advantages, depending on your project.

Pressing Seams to the Side: This is a common technique in quilting. Pressing seams to the side can add strength to the seam because the bulk of the fabric creates a sturdier edge. This method also helps reduce the likelihood of batting poking through the seams.

Tip: Press the seams toward the darker fabric to prevent shadows or fabric color showing through lighter blocks.

Pressing Seams Open: This method distributes the fabric evenly on both sides of the seam, which reduces bulk, especially at seam intersections. Pressing seams open can also help the quilt lay flatter.

Tip: If you're working with thicker batting or multiple layers, pressing seams open may be preferable to reduce the overall thickness of the quilt.

Use the Right Heat Setting

Different fabrics require different heat settings, so always adjust the temperature on your iron to suit the fabric you're working with.

Cotton Fabric: If you're working with 100% cotton, you can use a higher heat setting (usually "cotton" on the iron dial) to press your seams effectively. Cotton can handle higher temperatures, but make sure to avoid scorching by keeping the iron moving.

Blended Fabrics or Delicate Materials: For fabrics that contain synthetic fibers, use a lower heat setting to avoid melting or damaging the fabric. When in doubt, test the iron on a small scrap piece of fabric before pressing the quilt blocks.

Use Steam Carefully

Steam can be a helpful tool for pressing, but it must be used with care to avoid stretching or distorting your quilt blocks.

When to Use Steam: Steam is great for pressing stubborn wrinkles or creases. It can also help flatten seams more effectively when working with thicker materials or multiple layers of fabric and batting.

When to Avoid Steam: Too much steam can cause fabric to stretch, particularly lighter or loosely woven fabrics. If you notice distortion or stretching while pressing, switch to a dry press or use a light mist of water instead of full steam.

Press from the Front and Back

To achieve the best results, press your seams from both the front and back of the fabric.

Pressing from the Back: Start by pressing the seams from the back of the block, focusing on the seam allowances to flatten them properly.

Pressing from the Front: After pressing the back, turn the block over and press it from the front. This step smooths out any wrinkles and ensures a polished, flat finish.

Use a Pressing Cloth for Delicate Fabrics

If you're working with delicate fabrics or fabric blends that are sensitive to heat, use a pressing cloth between the fabric and the iron. A pressing cloth helps prevent scorching, shiny marks, or direct heat damage to the fabric.

How to Use a Pressing Cloth: Lay the pressing cloth over your quilt block, then press with the iron as usual. You can use a lightweight cotton cloth, muslin, or even a clean piece of scrap fabric for this purpose.

Set Seams Before Pressing Open

Before pressing your seams to one side or open, it's a good idea to set the seam by pressing it as sewn. This technique helps to embed the stitches into the fabric, which makes it easier to press the seam flat without creating distortion.

How to Set a Seam: After sewing a seam, place your iron on top of the seam without opening it up, and press. Then, proceed to open or press the seam to the side as needed.

Finger Pressing as You Sew

For smaller seams or areas where you need quick pressing, finger pressing can be effective. This technique involves using your fingers to flatten the seam without an iron, and it's useful for intricate piecing or when working with smaller blocks.

How to Finger Press: Run your fingers along the seam to open it up or press it to one side. While this method doesn't give as crisp of a finish as an iron, it helps to flatten seams temporarily before the final pressing.

Use a Tailor's Clapper for Flat Seams

A tailor's clapper is a wooden tool that helps set seams by absorbing heat and pressing the fabric flat. It's especially useful for thick or bulky seams that need extra pressure to stay flat.

How to Use a Clapper: After pressing your seam with an iron, place the clapper directly over the seam and press down. The clapper will help hold the heat in place, giving you a flatter, crisper seam.

Press Blocks After Quilting

After you've quilted your blocks in the QAYG method, press the entire block before joining it with other blocks. This will smooth out any wrinkles, and ensure that the blocks lie flat before piecing.

Pressing Quilt Sandwiches: Be mindful when pressing blocks that have been quilted with batting and backing. Use a dry iron or light steam if needed, but avoid applying too much pressure, as it can distort the quilted texture.

Trim Threads as You Press

As you press, take the opportunity to trim any loose threads around the seams or block edges. This keeps your work tidy and ensures that no stray threads get caught in your seams or show through on the front of the quilt.

Press Borders and Sashing

If your QAYG quilt includes borders or sashing between blocks, make sure to press these areas thoroughly to keep them smooth and prevent puckering.

Press Seams Toward the Sashing or Border: Press the seams of the blocks toward the sashing or border to reduce bulk in the quilt blocks themselves and give the quilt a more uniform appearance.

CHAPTER THREE
Basic Quilt as You Go (QAYG) Techniques

The Quilt as You Go (QAYG) method allows quilters to piece and quilt small sections of a project at a time, making the quilting process more manageable.

Traditional QAYG Method with Sashing

In the traditional QAYG method, blocks are quilted individually and then joined together with sashing strips, which hide the raw edges of the quilted blocks.

Materials Needed:

- Pre-cut quilt blocks (top fabric, batting, and backing)
- Sashing strips (for front and back)
- Sewing machine
- Pins or clips
- Quilting ruler and rotary cutter
- Iron

Step-by-Step Instructions:

Step 1: Prepare Your Blocks

Start by quilting each individual block. You'll have a "quilt sandwich" with the top fabric, batting, and backing for each block.

Quilt as desired (straight lines, free-motion quilting, etc.). Each block should be quilted to completion before moving on to the next step.

Step 2: Cut Sashing Strips

Cut sashing strips to the desired width (typically 1" to 1.5" wide) and the same length as your quilt blocks. You'll need two types of sashing:

Front Sashing: This will be visible on the front of your quilt.

Back Sashing: This will be visible on the back of your quilt.

Step 3: Attach Front Sashing

Take one of your quilted blocks and sew a front sashing strip to one edge, right sides together. Use a ¼" seam allowance.

Press the seam toward the sashing strip.

Step 4: Attach the Next Block

Lay the second quilted block on top of the sashing strip, aligning the edge of the block with the edge of the sashing (right sides together). Sew using a ¼" seam allowance.

Now, you should have two blocks joined by a sashing strip in the middle.

Step 5: Add Back Sashing

On the back of the quilt, sew a back sashing strip (cut slightly wider than the front strip) over the seam. Fold under the raw edge of the back sashing strip and topstitch it in place. This will encase the raw edges of the blocks and create a neat finish on the back.

Step 6: Repeat to Join All Blocks

Continue adding sashing strips to the front and back as you join more blocks. Follow the same process until all blocks are joined together.

Step 7: Finish with Borders (Optional)

If desired, add borders around the entire quilt using the same method (with sashing strips) to complete the project.

Join-and-Flip QAYG Method

The join-and-flip method is a simple and fast way to create a QAYG quilt without needing additional sashing strips. This method joins blocks as they are quilted and is ideal for strip quilts or log cabin designs.

Materials Needed:

- Pre-cut fabric strips (top fabric, batting, and backing)
- Sewing machine
- Pins or clips
- Quilting ruler and rotary cutter
- Iron

Step-by-Step Instructions:

Step 1: Prepare Your Fabric Strips

Cut fabric strips for the top of the quilt (2.5"-3" wide) and matching pieces of batting and backing. You can either pre-cut all your strips or cut them as you work through the quilt.

Lay your first strip of backing fabric down with the wrong side facing up. Place a strip of batting on top of it, aligning the edges.

Step 2: Attach the First Top Strip

Place the first strip of top fabric (right side up) on top of the batting. Pin or clip the three layers together: backing, batting, and top fabric.

Quilt this section as desired using straight or decorative stitches.

Step 3: Add the Next Strip

Place the second strip of top fabric on top of the first strip (right sides together), aligning the raw edges. The second strip should also be placed on top of the batting and backing.

Sew through all layers using a ¼" seam allowance along the raw edges of the strips.

Step 4: Flip and Press

Flip the second strip open so that the right side of the fabric is facing up, and press the seam flat.

Quilt along the second strip, just like you did with the first strip, using your preferred quilting design.

Step 5: Repeat the Process

Continue adding strips in the same manner, always sewing with right sides together, flipping, pressing, and quilting each new strip.

You'll be quilting the fabric, batting, and backing as you go, which means the quilted section grows with each new strip.

Step 6: Trim and Square the Quilt

Once you've added all the strips and quilted the entire piece, trim any excess batting or backing to square the edges of the quilt.

Step 7: Add Borders and Binding (Optional)

If desired, add borders to your quilt to frame the piece. Then, bind the edges to complete the quilt.

Lapped Seam QAYG Method

The lapped seam method is an easy way to join quilted blocks without the need for additional sashing. This method uses overlapping seams to create a clean finish.

Materials Needed:

- Pre-cut quilt blocks (top fabric, batting, and backing)
- Sewing machine
- Rotary cutter and quilting ruler
- Pins or clips
- Iron

Step-by-Step Instructions:

Step 1: Prepare Your Quilt Blocks

Quilt each block individually using your preferred quilting method, ensuring that each block is completed with batting and backing.

Step 2: Trim the Blocks

Trim each quilted block to ensure they are the same size. A typical size is 8" x 8" or 10" x 10," but you can choose any size for your project.

Step 3: Align the Blocks

Lay the first quilted block down with the right side facing up. Place the second quilted block on top of the first block, aligning the edges. The second block will overlap the first one by about ½".

Step 4: Pin the Blocks Together

Pin or clip the blocks in place to prevent shifting while sewing. Ensure that the overlapping area is secure.

Step 5: Sew the Lapped Seam

Sew along the edge of the top block where it overlaps the bottom block using a ¼" seam allowance. Be sure to backstitch at the beginning and end to secure the seam.

Step 6: Press the Seam

Press the seam toward the top block. This will help to keep the raw edges of the bottom block tucked underneath the top block.

Step 7: Repeat for Additional Blocks

Continue adding more quilted blocks in the same manner, overlapping each new block onto the previous one and securing with lapped seams. Press each seam as you go.

Step 8: Finish the Quilt

Once all blocks are joined together, trim any excess batting or backing as needed. You can add a border around the entire quilt if desired and finish with binding to complete the project.

Back to Front QAYG Method

The back-to-front method is a creative way to quilt and assemble your project simultaneously. In this technique, you sew the backing fabric to the top fabric and batting in one step, resulting in a clean finish on both sides of the quilt.

Materials Needed:

- Pre-cut quilt blocks (top fabric, batting, and backing)
- Sewing machine
- Rotary cutter and quilting ruler
- Pins or clips
- Iron

Step-by-Step Instructions:

Step 1: Prepare Your Fabric Pieces: Cut your top fabric, batting, and backing fabric into the desired size for your quilt blocks. You can choose any size, but a typical size is 10" x 10".

Step 2: Layer the Quilt Sandwich: Place the backing fabric wrong side up on your work surface. Next, lay the batting on top of the backing, ensuring it is centered.

Finally, place the top fabric right side up on top of the batting.

Step 3: Pin the Layers Together: Pin or clip the three layers together, making sure they are aligned and secure. This will help keep everything in place while you sew.

Step 4: Quilt the Layers: Quilt through all three layers as desired. You can use straight lines, free-motion quilting, or any design you like. Make sure to quilt the entire block.

Step 5: Trim Excess Fabric: After quilting, trim the excess backing and batting around the edges of the block to remove any unevenness. This will create a clean edge for joining blocks later.

Step 6: Repeat for Additional Blocks: Continue creating quilted blocks using the back-to-front method until you have the desired number of blocks for your quilt.

Step 7: Join the Blocks: To join the quilted blocks, place two blocks right sides together, aligning the edges. Pin in place, and sew along the edge using a ¼" seam allowance. Be sure to backstitch at the start and end.

Step 8: Flip and Press: Flip the blocks open so that the right sides are facing up. Press the seams to one side or open, depending on your preference.

Step 9: Finish the Quilt: Continue joining blocks until the quilt top is complete. You can add borders if desired, and finish with binding to complete your quilt.

CHAPTER FOUR
Advanced QAYG Technique

Crisscross QAYG Method

The crisscross method is an advanced technique that allows you to create intricate quilt designs with intersecting lines, giving your quilt a dynamic look. This technique combines piecing and quilting in a visually appealing way.

Materials Needed:

- Pre-cut fabric squares (top fabric, batting, and backing)
- Sewing machine
- Rotary cutter and quilting ruler
- Pins or clips
- Iron
- Marking tool (for drawing guidelines)

Step-by-Step Instructions:

Step 1: Prepare Your Fabric Squares: Cut your fabric squares for the top, batting, and backing. A typical size is 10" x 10". Ensure that you have enough squares for the desired quilt size.

Step 2: Mark Your Quilting Lines: For each square, use a marking tool to draw guidelines on the top fabric. Draw diagonal lines from corner to corner, creating an "X" shape on each square.

Step 3: Layer the Quilt Sandwich: Layer each square by placing the backing fabric right side down, followed by the batting, and finally the top fabric with the marked lines facing up.

Step 4: Pin the Layers Together: Pin or clip the layers to hold them in place while sewing. Make sure the layers are aligned correctly.

Step 5: Quilt Along the Marked Lines: Sew along the marked diagonal lines to create the crisscross pattern. Start from one corner and sew to the opposite corner, then repeat for the other diagonal. You can choose to quilt additional lines if desired.

Step 6: Trim the Squares: After quilting, trim the excess backing and batting around the edges of the square to create a clean finish.

Step 7: Join the Squares: Lay two quilted squares right sides together, aligning the edges. Pin in place and sew along one edge using a ¼" seam allowance. Repeat to join additional squares, ensuring the crisscross pattern remains consistent.

Step 8: Flip and Press: Flip the joined squares open, so the right sides are facing up. Press the seams to one side or open as desired.

Step 9: Finish the Quilt: Continue joining squares until the quilt top is complete. Add borders if desired, and finish with binding to complete your quilt.

Curved QAYG Method

The curved QAYG method allows quilters to create quilts with soft, flowing lines instead of straight edges. This technique is ideal for creating a more organic, artistic design in your quilts.

Materials Needed:

- Pre-cut fabric pieces (top fabric, batting, and backing)
- Sewing machine
- Rotary cutter and quilting ruler
- Pins or clips
- Iron
- Template for curves (can be made from cardboard or plastic)

Step-by-Step Instructions:

Step 1: Prepare Your Fabric Pieces: Cut your top fabric, batting, and backing into various shapes, such as curved pieces or arcs. You can use a template to achieve consistent curves. Aim for a range of sizes for a more dynamic look.

Step 2: Layer the Quilt Sandwich: Lay the backing fabric right side down, followed by the batting, and then the top fabric piece with the right side facing up.

Step 3: Pin the Layers Together: Pin or clip the layers in place to secure them for sewing.

Step 4: Sew the Curved Edges: Using a sewing machine, sew along the curved edges of the top fabric. Use a walking foot if available, as it helps manage the layers better. Start slowly, and adjust the fabric as needed to maintain the curve.

Step 5: Trim the Excess: Trim any excess batting and backing fabric along the edges, ensuring a clean finish.

Step 6: Add Additional Curved Pieces: To add more pieces, place a new curved top fabric piece right sides together with the previous piece, aligning the edges. Pin and sew along the curved seam, following the same technique as before.

Step 7: Flip and Press: After sewing, flip the new piece open to reveal the curve. Press the seam allowances toward the new piece to create a clean edge.

Step 8: Continue Adding Pieces: Repeat the process of adding curved pieces, layering and sewing until the desired quilt size is achieved.

Step 9: Finish the Quilt: Once all pieces are joined, add borders if desired, and finish with binding to complete your quilt.

Sashiko QAYG Method

The Sashiko QAYG method combines traditional Japanese Sashiko stitching with the Quilt as You Go technique. This method not only provides a functional way to quilt but also adds beautiful decorative stitching to your project.

Materials Needed:

- Pre-cut fabric squares (top fabric, batting, and backing)
- Sewing machine

- Sashiko thread or regular quilting thread
- Hand sewing needle (for Sashiko)
- Rotary cutter and quilting ruler
- Pins or clips
- Iron
- Sashiko stencil or marking tool

Step-by-Step Instructions:

Step 1: Prepare Your Fabric Squares: Cut your top fabric, batting, and backing into the desired size for your quilt squares, typically 10" x 10".

Step 2: Mark the Sashiko Design: Using a Sashiko stencil or a marking tool, draw your desired Sashiko pattern onto the top fabric. Traditional Sashiko patterns often include geometric shapes and repetitive designs.

Step 3: Layer the Quilt Sandwich: Layer each square by placing the backing fabric right side down, followed by the batting, and finally the top fabric with the marked Sashiko design facing up.

Step 4: Pin the Layers Together: Pin or clip the layers to hold them in place while you sew.

Step 5: Quilt the Layers: Using your sewing machine, quilt along the edges of the Sashiko design to secure the layers. This will also outline the Sashiko pattern.

Step 6: Hand Stitch Sashiko: Thread your hand sewing needle with Sashiko thread and use a simple running stitch to sew along the marked lines of your Sashiko design. Use even stitches for a clean, traditional look.

Step 7: Trim the Squares: After completing the Sashiko stitching, trim the excess backing and batting around the edges of the square to create a clean finish.

Step 8: Join the Squares: Lay two quilted squares right sides together, aligning the edges. Pin in place and sew along one edge using a ¼" seam allowance. Repeat to join additional squares.

Step 9: Flip and Press: Flip the joined squares open, so the right sides are facing up. Press the seams to one side or open, as desired.

Step 10: Finish the Quilt: Continue joining squares until the quilt top is complete. Add borders if desired, and finish with binding to complete your quilt.

Asymmetrical QAYG Method

The asymmetrical QAYG method allows for creative freedom by encouraging the use of uneven blocks and irregular shapes. This method creates a modern look and unique design.

Materials Needed:

- Various pre-cut fabric pieces (top fabric, batting, and backing)
- Sewing machine
- Rotary cutter and quilting ruler
- Pins or clips
- Iron
- Design board or large surface for layout

Step-by-Step Instructions:

Step 1: Prepare Your Fabric Pieces: Cut a variety of fabric pieces into irregular shapes, such as triangles, rectangles, and other geometric forms. You can also use leftover fabric scraps for this method.

Step 2: Plan Your Layout: On a design board or large surface, arrange your fabric pieces to create an asymmetrical design.

Experiment with colors and shapes until you achieve a layout you like.

Step 3: Layer the Quilt Sandwich: For each piece, layer the backing fabric right side down, followed by the batting, and then the top fabric with the right side facing up. Ensure each piece is the desired size to fit into your layout.

Step 4: Pin the Layers Together: Pin or clip the layers in place to secure them for sewing.

Step 5: Quilt Each Piece: Using your sewing machine, quilt through all three layers, following the edges of the top fabric. You can choose to do free-motion quilting or simple straight-line quilting, depending on your design.

Step 6: Trim the Edges: After quilting, trim any excess backing and batting along the edges of each piece for a clean finish.

Step 7: Join the Pieces: Lay two quilted pieces right sides together, aligning the edges. Pin in place and sew along one edge using a ¼" seam allowance. Repeat to join additional pieces, ensuring the asymmetrical design is maintained.

Step 8: Flip and Press: After sewing, flip the joined pieces open and press the seams to one side or open.

Step 9: Continue Adding Pieces: Continue joining pieces until the quilt top is complete. You can create interesting overlaps and angles for added visual interest.

Step 10: Finish the Quilt: Once all pieces are joined, add borders if desired, and finish with binding to complete your quilt.

CHAPTER FIVE
Designing Your Quilt

Planning Your Layout

Planning your layout is a crucial step in the Quilt as You Go (QAYG) process. It sets the stage for your quilt's overall design and ensures that all pieces fit together harmoniously.

Choose a Theme or Design Style

Inspiration: Start by selecting a theme or style for your quilt. This could be based on color palettes, patterns, or specific motifs (e.g., floral, geometric, modern, or traditional).

Mood Board: Create a mood board with fabric swatches, images, and color schemes that resonate with your theme. This can help visualize your overall design.

Select Your Fabric

Color Coordination: Choose fabrics that complement each other and align with your chosen theme. Consider using a mix of prints, solids, and textures to add depth to your quilt.

Fabric Amounts: Determine how much fabric you'll need for your blocks, borders, and backing. Having a variety of options will allow for more creative freedom during layout.

Decide on Block Sizes and Shapes

Standard vs. Unique Shapes: Decide if you want to use standard block sizes (e.g., 10" squares) or experiment with unique shapes (e.g., triangles, curves, or irregular shapes).

Consistent Sizing: If you opt for standard sizes, make sure all blocks are cut consistently for easier assembly. For unique shapes, ensure they can be joined seamlessly.

Arrange Your Blocks

Design Surface: Use a large design board, wall, or floor space to lay out your blocks. This will give you a clearer view of the overall layout and allow for easy rearrangement.

Experiment with Placement: Start by arranging blocks in different configurations. Consider alternating colors, patterns, and shapes to create visual interest.

Consider Balance: Aim for a balanced look by distributing colors and patterns evenly across the quilt. Avoid clustering similar fabrics together unless it serves a specific design purpose.

Use Design Software (Optional)

Digital Tools: If you prefer a more technical approach, consider using quilt design software or apps. These tools allow you to create digital layouts, making it easier to visualize your quilt before cutting and sewing.

Plan Borders and Sashing

Borders: Decide if you want to add borders around your quilt. Borders can frame your design and add structure.

Sashing: Consider using sashing (strips of fabric between blocks) to create separation and enhance the overall design. Choose a fabric that complements your blocks without overpowering them.

Take Photos

Visual Reference: Once you're happy with your layout, take photos of your arrangement. This can serve as a reference while you sew and helps keep the layout consistent.

Finalize the Layout

Review and Adjust: Take a step back and review your layout from different angles. Make any final adjustments to ensure you are satisfied with the overall look.

Document Your Plan: Write down the sizes and placements of your blocks, especially if you're using a complex arrangement. This will guide you as you assemble your quilt.

Prepare for Assembly

Label Blocks: If your quilt layout is intricate, consider labeling each block or keeping a numbered list. This can prevent confusion during assembly.

Cutting Order: Plan the order in which you will cut and sew your blocks based on your layout, ensuring a smooth assembly process.

Start Sewing

Once your layout is finalized and documented, you're ready to start the QAYG process. Assemble your quilt blocks according to your planned layout, following your chosen techniques.

Color Theory and Fabric Selection

Understanding color theory and fabric selection is vital for creating visually appealing quilts, especially in a Quilt as You Go (QAYG) project.

Basics of Color Theory

Color Wheel

Primary Colors: Red, blue, and yellow. These cannot be created by mixing other colors.

Secondary Colors: Green, orange, and purple, formed by mixing two primary colors.

Tertiary Colors: Created by mixing a primary color with a secondary color (e.g., red-orange).

Color Harmonies

Complementary Colors: Colors that are opposite each other on the color wheel (e.g., blue and orange). These create high contrast and vibrant designs.

Analogous Colors: Colors that are next to each other on the color wheel (e.g., blue,

blue-green, and green). These create a harmonious and soothing effect.

Triadic Colors: A set of three colors evenly spaced around the color wheel (e.g., red, yellow, and blue). This scheme offers a balanced and vibrant look.

Monochromatic Colors: Variations of one color in different shades and tints. This creates a cohesive and unified design.

Choosing a Color Palette

Inspiration Sources

Nature: Look at landscapes, flowers, and seasons for natural color combinations.

Art: Draw inspiration from paintings, textiles, and crafts.

Fashion: Consider current trends in fashion for fresh color ideas.

Creating a Palette

Limit Your Colors: Start with 3 to 5 colors to avoid overwhelming your design.

Choose a Dominant Color: Select one color to dominate your quilt, and use others as accents.

Consider Contrast: Ensure there's enough contrast between fabrics to highlight patterns and shapes.

Fabric Selection

Fabric Types

Cotton: The most common choice for quilting due to its durability, versatility, and ease of handling.

Batiks: Hand-dyed fabrics with vibrant colors and patterns, adding unique texture.

Flannel: Soft and cozy, great for warmer quilts but can add bulk.

Voile or Lawn: Lightweight and sheer, ideal for soft, flowing quilts.

Fabric Patterns

Solids: Solid colors can create a clean look and make prints pop.

Prints: Choose prints that complement your color palette. Large prints can serve as focal points, while small prints add texture without overwhelming the design.

Texture: Consider using textured fabrics (e.g., corduroy, linen) to add depth to your quilt.

Fabric Selection Tips

Test Swatches: Before committing to a fabric, buy swatches to test how colors look together. Lay them out in your planned layout to see how they interact.

Lighting: Evaluate fabrics in natural light to see their true colors. Indoor lighting can alter how colors appear.

Mixing Patterns: Combine different pattern scales (e.g., small florals with larger geometric prints) for added interest.

Ensure that busy fabrics are balanced with simpler ones to avoid visual chaos.

Consider the Overall Mood

Warm Colors: (reds, oranges, yellows) evoke warmth and energy. Great for vibrant, lively quilts.

Cool Colors: (blues, greens, purples) create a calm and soothing effect, suitable for serene or restful designs.

Neutral Colors: (whites, grays, beiges) can help balance bright colors and provide a background for other fabrics.

Personal Style and Preference

Reflect Your Personality: Choose fabrics and colors that resonate with you. Personal preference is crucial in creating a quilt that you love.

Experiment: Don't hesitate to try unexpected combinations. Sometimes, the best designs come from adventurous color choices.

Tips For Creating Cohesive Designs

Creating cohesive designs in quilting, particularly in Quilt as You Go (QAYG) projects, is essential for ensuring that your quilt looks well-balanced and visually appealing.

Stick to a Consistent Color Palette

Limit Your Color Scheme: Choose 3-5 colors that complement each other. A limited palette helps avoid visual chaos and gives your quilt a more intentional and cohesive look.

Use a Dominant Color: Choose one color to be dominant throughout the quilt. This can act as a unifying element across all blocks, tying them together.

Accent Colors: Use accent colors sparingly to add interest, but ensure they fit within the overall palette.

Balance Patterns and Solids

Mix Prints and Solids: Combining patterned fabrics with solid colors creates a balanced design. Use solids to break up busy prints and provide resting points for the eye.

Scale of Prints: Vary the scale of patterns (small, medium, and large) to create visual interest without overwhelming the design. Too many large prints can clash, while too many small ones may look monotonous.

Maintain Consistent Block Sizes

Uniformity in Blocks: Keep your blocks the same size throughout the quilt. Consistency in block size helps create a clean, structured appearance that enhances cohesion.

Symmetry: If using blocks of different shapes or sizes, arrange them in a symmetrical or balanced manner for a more organized look.

Use Repeating Motifs

Repeated Patterns: Repeating certain motifs or shapes in multiple blocks can tie the design together. This could be a specific quilting pattern, appliqué, or type of block.

Echo Shapes: Consider using similar shapes or elements across your blocks. For example, if you feature stars in one block, echo that shape in other areas of your quilt to create a visual rhythm.

Plan a Structured Layout

Grid Layout: A grid layout helps to create a more cohesive appearance by organizing your blocks in a clear, structured format. It also gives a sense of order, even if the blocks themselves have varied patterns.

Consistent Spacing: Use consistent spacing between blocks and rows to give the quilt a unified, professional finish.

Borders and Sashing: Consider adding borders or sashing (fabric strips between blocks) to separate the blocks and unify the design. Sashing in a neutral or coordinating color can tie together different blocks while giving each its own space.

Use a Common Fabric or Theme

Unifying Fabric: Incorporate a common fabric throughout your quilt, either as a background or a part of each block. This gives the quilt a cohesive thread that runs through the design.

Theme or Concept: Stick to a specific theme, such as floral, geometric, or holiday, and select fabrics and blocks that align with that concept.

Pay Attention to Contrast

Contrast for Definition: Use contrasting colors or values (light vs. dark) to define your blocks clearly. This creates visual interest and helps your design elements stand out.

Balance of Contrast: Ensure that your quilt has both high-contrast and low-contrast areas to keep the eye moving across the design. Too much contrast can be overwhelming, while too little can make the quilt look flat.

Focus on a Focal Point

Feature Block: Create a focal point by designing one or more standout blocks that draw attention. These can be larger, more detailed, or feature bold colors.

Supporting Blocks: Design surrounding blocks to complement but not compete with the focal point. This helps create balance while still highlighting your feature block.

Edit and Simplify

Avoid Overcomplication: It's easy to get carried away with adding too many fabrics, patterns, or techniques. Simplify your design by removing elements that feel unnecessary or don't contribute to the overall harmony of the quilt.

Cohesion Over Complexity: Focus on how the individual blocks work together as a whole, rather than making each block highly detailed or intricate. A simple, cohesive design can often be more impactful than a complex, disjointed one.

Trust Your Gut

Personal Aesthetic: While rules of color theory and design are helpful, trust your instincts. If something looks off to you, adjust it. If it feels right, go with it. Your personal touch is what makes your quilt unique.

Step Back: Periodically take a step back from your quilt and view it from a distance. This gives you a fresh perspective on whether the design feels balanced and cohesive.

Adding Backing and Binding

Adding backing and binding to a Quilt as You Go (QAYG) project is one of the final steps to completing your quilt. These finishing touches ensure your quilt looks polished and professional.

Preparing the Backing

Choose the Right Fabric

Fabric Selection: The backing fabric should complement your quilt top. You can choose a solid color, a patterned fabric, or even piece together leftover fabrics from the front.

Size Consideration: Make sure the backing fabric is at least 2-4 inches larger than the quilt top on all sides. This extra allowance ensures you have enough fabric to cover any shifting that occurs during quilting.

Cut and Piece the Backing

Cutting: If your quilt is larger than the width of your backing fabric, you may need to piece multiple fabric panels together.

Sew them with a 1/4-inch seam allowance, and press the seams open to reduce bulk.

Lay Out the Backing: Lay the backing fabric flat, with the wrong side facing up. Smooth out any wrinkles.

Layering the Quilt

Layering Order: Place the quilt top on the backing fabric with the right side facing up. If your quilt has batting, layer the batting between the quilt top and the backing. Smooth out the quilt top to ensure it lies flat without any puckering.

Pin or Baste: Use safety pins or basting spray to secure the layers together. Start from the center and work your way outward to avoid wrinkles or folds.

Adding the Binding

Cutting the Binding

Fabric Choice: Choose a binding fabric that complements or contrasts with your quilt's design.

Binding Strips: Cut strips of fabric 2.5 to 3 inches wide, depending on your preference for binding width. If your quilt has curved edges, cut the strips on the bias (diagonal to the fabric's grain). For straight edges, you can cut them along the fabric's width or length.

Joining Strips: If you need longer binding, join multiple strips. To do this, place two strips at a 90-degree angle with right sides together, and sew diagonally from one corner to the other. Trim the excess fabric to leave a 1/4-inch seam allowance, and press the seam open.

Attaching the Binding

Machine Sew the Binding: Start by placing the binding on the front side of the quilt with the raw edges aligned.

Leave a 6-8 inch tail of binding unsewn at the beginning. Sew the binding using a 1/4-inch seam allowance.

When you reach a corner, stop 1/4 inch from the edge, and fold the binding up at a 45-degree angle, then fold it back down in line with the next edge. This will create a mitered corner.

Continue sewing along the next edge, repeating this process at each corner.

Joining the Binding Ends

Final Seam: When you reach the point where you started, overlap the binding ends. Open the binding tails, place them right sides together, and sew diagonally to join them. Trim the excess fabric, and finish sewing the binding to the quilt.

Press and Finish

Pressing: Once the binding is attached, press the quilt to smooth out any wrinkles. Pay extra attention to the edges and corners to ensure a clean, professional finish.

Trim Any Loose Threads: Inspect the quilt for any stray threads or uneven stitches, and trim them for a tidy result.

Final Touches and Embellishments

Adding final touches and embellishments to your Quilt as You Go (QAYG) project is the perfect way to personalize and enhance its overall aesthetic. These finishing details can transform a simple quilt into a unique piece of art.

Adding Embellishments

Appliqué: Appliqué involves sewing pieces of fabric onto the quilt top to create designs or patterns.

How to Apply: You can hand-stitch or machine-stitch appliqué pieces. For a cleaner edge, use a fusible web to adhere the fabric shapes before stitching them down with a blanket stitch or zigzag stitch.

Design Ideas: Try adding flowers, shapes, or motifs that complement your quilt theme. This technique can be used sparingly to accent certain blocks or all over the quilt for a more intricate look.

Embroidery

Hand Embroidery: Add hand-stitched details like names, quotes, or decorative patterns to individual blocks. Use embroidery floss and a variety of stitches like backstitch, French knots, or satin stitch for texture and visual interest.

Machine Embroidery: If you have an embroidery machine, you can add detailed designs before or after piecing the blocks together. This technique can make your quilt stand out with intricate motifs and embellishments.

Beading

Add Dimension: Beads can be sewn onto individual quilt blocks for a bit of sparkle and texture. Choose beads that complement your quilt's colors and design. Sew them in clusters or in specific patterns to enhance the overall visual appeal.

Sturdy Beads: Ensure the beads you choose aren't too heavy or sharp to avoid damaging the fabric. They should also be securely fastened to withstand washing.

Buttons

Creative Accents: Buttons can add a whimsical or decorative touch to your quilt. Use them to highlight specific areas, like the center of a flower appliqué or in a grid pattern on a block. Choose buttons that complement the quilt's color scheme and theme.

Sew Securely: Be sure to sew buttons securely, especially if the quilt will be used frequently or washed often.

Decorative Stitching

Hand Quilting Details

Big Stitch Quilting: This technique uses larger stitches with thicker thread (like embroidery floss or perle cotton) to create a bold, decorative look. Choose contrasting colors to make the stitches stand out.

Echo Quilting: Hand quilt around appliqué shapes or embroidered designs to make them pop. This technique adds dimension and focuses attention on the key elements of the quilt.

Machine Quilting Details

Free-Motion Quilting Patterns: Use free-motion quilting to add detailed designs such as flowers, leaves, or swirls around blocks. This adds an artistic flair and enhances the overall texture of the quilt.

Contrasting Thread: Consider using a contrasting thread color to make your quilting stitches more noticeable, turning them into a decorative element.

Binding Enhancements

Decorative Binding

Use Patterned Fabric: Instead of plain binding, choose a patterned or contrasting fabric to make the edges of your quilt stand out.

Piped Binding: Add piping inside the binding for a more polished, professional finish. This adds a pop of color or texture around the quilt's edges.

Scalloped or Shaped Edges

Scalloped Edges: For a more decorative look, cut the edges of your quilt into scalloped or wavy shapes before adding the binding. This gives a more delicate and unique finish to the quilt.

Curved Binding: Curved edges require bias binding, which stretches around the curves without puckering. This technique is a bit more advanced but adds elegance to the final product.

Personal Labels

Quilt Labels

Personalize Your Quilt: Adding a personalized quilt label is a thoughtful way to commemorate the quilt. Include details like the quilt's name, the maker's name, the date, or a special message.

Sew-in Label: Create or purchase a fabric label and sew it onto the back of your quilt. You can hand-stitch it in place for a more personal touch, or machine-stitch for a more durable finish.

Embroidered Label: If you enjoy embroidery, consider stitching the label by hand. This adds a unique, handmade feel that enhances the quilt's story.

Custom Stamping or Printing

Fabric Markers or Stamps: Use fabric markers or stamps to create a label directly on the backing fabric. Make sure the ink is washable and fabric-safe.

Print-on-Fabric Labels: Print your label using inkjet fabric sheets that can be sewn onto your quilt. This allows you to include a detailed message or design on the label.

Decorative Binding Stitches

Decorative Stitches: When sewing the binding, use a decorative machine stitch such as a blanket stitch, zigzag, or scallop to add flair to the edges.

Contrasting Thread: Use a thread color that contrasts with the binding fabric to make the stitching pop. This turns your binding into a decorative element that complements the overall design.

Fringe or Tassels

Tassels or Fringe: For a bohemian or playful touch, consider adding fringe or tassels to the edges of the quilt. These can be sewn into the binding or attached afterward.

Materials: Use yarn, embroidery floss, or fabric scraps to create tassels or fringe that complement the quilt's colors and style.

Fabric Paints or Ink

Hand-Painted Details: If you want to add a truly unique touch, consider using fabric paints or ink to create custom designs on your quilt. This can include patterns, quotes, or small artistic accents on the blocks.

Stenciling: Use stencils and fabric-safe paint to add designs without the need for embroidery or appliqué. Stenciled motifs can be added to plain blocks or used to complement pieced designs.

Final Touches to Keep in Mind

Balance the Embellishments: While embellishments add a lot of character to a quilt, it's important not to overdo it. Choose a few key areas to highlight without overwhelming the overall design.

Durability Considerations: If the quilt will be used frequently or washed often, ensure the embellishments are securely attached and durable enough to withstand wear and tear.

Personalization: The final touches are where your creativity shines the most. Personalize the quilt with designs, colors, and embellishments that reflect the intended recipient or your personal style.

CHAPTER SIX
Beginner Qayg Projects

QAYG Coasters

Materials:

- Fabric scraps (for quilt top)
- Batting (cotton or polyester, cut to 4" x 4")
- Backing fabric (cut to 4" x 4")
- Thread (to match or contrast with fabric)
- Sewing machine (optional for hand stitching)

Steps:

Cut Fabric Strips: Cut your fabric scraps into strips about 1" to 1.5" wide. Length can vary, but aim for around 5"-7" long for each strip.

Layer Batting and Backing: Place your batting square on top of your backing fabric square, wrong side of the fabric facing down.

Attach the First Fabric Strip: Place your first fabric strip right-side-up on the batting. Center it or place it toward one side of the coaster as a starting point.

Add the Second Strip: Take the second fabric strip and place it right-side-down, aligning it with one edge of the first strip. Sew a ¼" seam along the aligned edge, attaching the two strips to the batting and backing fabric.

Press Open: After sewing, flip the second strip right-side-up and press it open using an iron. This ensures a neat finish and prepares it for the next strip.

Repeat the Process: Continue adding strips of fabric in the same manner, sewing, flipping, and pressing each one until the entire square is covered. Trim any excess fabric hanging over the edges.

Top Stitch (Optional): You can add decorative top stitching along the seams of each strip for added detail and durability.

Finish the Edges: Trim the coaster to a neat square, if necessary, and finish the edges by either adding a binding or simply using a zigzag stitch to secure and prevent fraying.

QAYG Placemat

Materials:

- Fabric scraps or fat quarters

- Batting (cut to placemat size, 12" x 18" or preferred size)
- Backing fabric (cut to match the size of the batting)
- Thread
- Sewing machine

Steps:

Prepare the Batting and Backing: Place your batting on top of the backing fabric, making sure the wrong side of the backing is facing down. Smooth out any wrinkles.

Cut Fabric Strips: Cut your fabric scraps or fat quarters into strips that are 2" to 2.5" wide. Vary the length of the strips to add interest to the design.

Attach the First Strip: Place the first fabric strip right-side-up along one edge of the batting. Align it with the edge and secure it with pins, if needed.

Sew the Second Strip: Take the second strip and place it right-side-down on top of the first strip, aligning the edges. Sew a ¼" seam along the edge where the two strips meet.

Press Open: Flip the second strip right-side-up and press it flat with an iron.

Continue Adding Strips: Repeat the process of adding strips, sewing, flipping, and pressing each one until you cover the entire placemat with fabric. Trim any overhanging fabric to keep the edges clean.

Quilt the Top (Optional): If you'd like to add more texture or quilting, stitch in the ditch along the seams of the fabric strips or create additional quilting lines.

Finish with Binding: To finish the placemat, add binding around the edges. Cut 2.5" wide binding strips, sew them around the perimeter of the placemat, and fold them over the edges for a clean finish.

QAYG Zipper Pouch

Materials:

- Fabric scraps for quilt top
- Batting (cut to pouch size, typically 8" x 10" or preferred size)
- Lining fabric (same size as batting)
- Zipper (8" or longer)
- Thread
- Sewing machine

Steps:

Cut Fabric Strips: Cut your fabric scraps into strips about 1" to 2" wide. You can vary the lengths based on how you want the design to look.

Layer Batting and Lining: Place your batting piece on top of the lining fabric, wrong side of the lining facing down.

Attach the First Strip: Place the first strip of fabric right-side-up at one end of the batting. Pin or secure it in place.

Add the Next Strip: Place the second strip right-side-down on top of the first strip, align the edges, and sew a ¼" seam along the edge where the strips meet.

Flip and Press: Flip the second strip right-side-up and press it flat with an iron.

Continue Adding Strips: Repeat the process of adding strips, sewing, flipping, and pressing until the entire batting piece is covered. Trim any excess fabric.

Quilt the Pouch (Optional): You can add additional quilting lines to secure the fabric strips to the batting for a more textured look.

Sew the Zipper: Place the zipper face down along the top edge of the quilted fabric. Attach the zipper using a zipper foot on your sewing machine. Then, sew the other side of the zipper to the lining.

Assemble the Pouch: Fold the quilted piece in half with the zipper centered on top. Sew the side seams, making sure to leave the zipper slightly open to turn the pouch right-side-out.

Finish the Edges: Trim any excess fabric and finish the edges by zigzag stitching or using a serger to prevent fraying.

QAYG Table Runner

Materials:

- Fabric scraps or fat quarters for quilt top
- Batting (cut to table runner size, typically 12" x 36")

- Backing fabric (cut to match the size of the batting)
- Thread
- Sewing machine

Steps:

Prepare Batting and Backing: Lay your batting on top of the backing fabric, ensuring the wrong side of the backing faces down. Smooth out any wrinkles.

Cut Fabric Strips or Squares: Cut your fabric scraps into strips or squares, depending on the design you want for the table runner. Strips should be 2" to 3" wide, while squares can be about 5" x 5".

Attach the First Piece: Place the first strip or square right-side-up on one end of the batting, securing it with pins if necessary.

Sew the Second Piece: Place the next strip or square right-side-down on top of the first piece, aligning the edges. Sew a ¼" seam along the aligned edges.

Flip and Press: Flip the second piece right-side-up and press it with an iron.

Continue Adding Pieces: Repeat the process of sewing, flipping, and pressing until the entire table runner is covered with fabric strips or squares.

Quilt the Top (Optional): Add quilting lines along the seams or in between the strips to give your table runner more texture and durability.

Finish with Binding: Once the top is complete, add binding around the edges to give the table runner a polished finish. Cut 2.5" wide binding strips and sew them around the edges.

QAYG Mug Rug

Materials:

- Fabric scraps or charm squares (5" x 5")
- Batting (cut to 6" x 9" or preferred size)
- Backing fabric (cut to match the size of the batting)
- Thread
- Sewing machine

Steps:

Prepare Your Fabric: Gather your fabric scraps or charm squares. You can use a mix of different fabrics for a patchwork effect.

Layer Batting and Backing: Place your batting on a flat surface, then place the backing fabric on top of it, wrong side facing up.

Arrange Fabric Squares: Lay out your fabric squares or strips on top of the batting in the arrangement you prefer. This will be the top of your mug rug.

Attach the First Square: Place the first fabric square right-side-up on one end of the batting. Secure it with pins if needed.

Sew the Next Square: Take the second fabric square and place it right-side-down on the first square, aligning the edges. Sew a ¼" seam along the edge where they meet.

Flip and Press: Flip the second square right-side-up and press it flat with an iron.

Continue Adding Squares: Repeat the process of adding squares until you've covered the entire batting area. Trim any excess fabric if necessary.

Quilt the Mug Rug: To add texture, sew along the seams or create additional quilting lines on the mug rug's surface.

Finish with Backing: To finish, trim the edges of the mug rug to make them even, then layer the backing fabric on top of the quilted piece, right sides together. Sew around the edges, leaving an opening to turn it right-side-out.

Turn and Finish: Turn the mug rug right-side-out through the opening, press flat, and topstitch around the edges to close the opening.

QAYG Baby Blanket

Materials:

- Fabric scraps or fat quarters for quilt top
- Batting (cut to desired blanket size, typically 36" x 36" or preferred size)
- Backing fabric (cut to match the size of the batting)
- Thread
- Sewing machine

Steps:

Prepare Your Fabrics: Gather a variety of fabric scraps or fat quarters in playful colors and patterns suitable for a baby blanket.

Layer Batting and Backing: Place the batting on a flat surface, then lay the backing fabric on top, wrong side facing down.

Cut Fabric Pieces: Cut fabric scraps into strips or squares, about 4" to 6" wide.

Attach the First Piece: Place the first fabric piece right-side-up at one corner of the batting.

Add the Next Piece: Place the second piece right-side-down on top of the first piece, aligning the edges. Sew a ¼" seam along the edge.

Flip and Press: Flip the second piece right-side-up and press it flat with an iron.

Continue Adding Pieces: Repeat the process of sewing, flipping, and pressing until the entire batting area is covered with fabric.

Quilt the Blanket: Optionally, quilt along the seams or create additional quilting lines throughout the blanket for added texture.

Finish with Backing: Trim the edges of the quilted top if necessary, then layer the backing fabric on top of the quilted top, right sides together. Sew around the edges, leaving an opening.

Turn and Finish: Turn the blanket right-side-out through the opening, press it flat, and topstitch around the edges to close the opening.

CHAPTER SEVEN
Intermediate QAYG Projects

QAYG Patchwork Tote Bag

Materials:

- Fabric scraps or fat quarters for the exterior
- Lining fabric
- Batting (cut to the size of the bag pieces, typically 18" x 22" for exterior and lining)
- Straps (can be made from fabric or purchased)
- Thread
- Sewing machine

Steps:

Prepare Your Fabric: Cut your fabric scraps into squares or strips (3" to 5") for the exterior of the tote bag. You will need enough pieces to cover the batting.

Layer Batting and Lining: Cut the batting to match the size of the tote bag pieces (18" x 22"). Layer the batting on a flat surface, followed by the lining fabric, wrong side facing up.

Arrange Fabric Pieces: Lay out your fabric squares or strips on top of the batting in a design that you like.

Attach the First Piece: Place the first fabric piece right-side-up at one edge of the batting. Pin it in place.

Sew the Next Piece: Place the second piece right-side-down on top of the first piece, aligning the edges. Sew a ¼" seam along the edge where they meet.

Flip and Press: Flip the second piece right-side-up and press it flat with an iron. Continue adding fabric pieces until the entire batting is covered. Trim any excess fabric.

Quilt the Tote: Optionally, quilt along the seams or create additional quilting lines to secure the fabric to the batting.

Cut Lining and Assembly: Cut a matching piece of lining fabric and attach it to the tote bag exterior. With right sides together, sew along the edges, leaving the top open.

Create the Straps: Cut fabric strips for the straps (about 2" wide). Fold and press, then sew along the edges. Attach the straps to the top edge of the tote bag, securing them in place.

Finish the Tote Bag: Fold the bag with right sides together and sew along the sides and bottom. Turn it right-side-out, press, and your patchwork tote bag is ready!

QAYG Wall Hanging Quilt

Materials:

- Fabric scraps in various colors and patterns
- Batting (cut to desired wall hanging size, typically 24" x 36")
- Backing fabric (cut to match the size of the batting)
- Thread
- Wooden dowel or hanger for display
- Sewing machine

Steps:

Prepare Your Fabric: Cut your fabric scraps into squares, triangles, or strips, depending on your desired design (2" to 6" pieces work well).

Layer Batting and Backing: Cut the batting to your chosen wall hanging size (24" x 36"). Place the batting on a flat surface, then place the backing fabric on top, wrong side facing down.

Design the Layout: Arrange your fabric pieces on top of the batting in a pattern that you like. This can be a geometric design or a random patchwork.

Attach the First Piece: Place the first fabric piece right-side-up at one corner of the batting.

Sew the Next Piece: Place the next piece right-side-down on top of the first piece, aligning the edges. Sew a ¼" seam along the edge.

Flip and Press: Flip the second piece right-side-up and press it with an iron. Continue adding pieces until the batting is fully covered, trimming any excess fabric as needed.

Quilt the Wall Hanging: Once the top is complete, quilt along the seams or add decorative quilting lines to enhance the design.

Add the Backing: Cut a piece of backing fabric to match the size of the wall hanging. Layer it on top of the quilted piece, right sides together. Sew around the edges, leaving an opening for turning.

Turn and Finish: Turn the wall hanging right-side-out through the opening. Press it flat, ensuring the edges are neat. Topstitch around the perimeter to close the opening.

Attach the Hanging Mechanism: Sew a pocket or loop at the top of the wall hanging for a wooden dowel or hanger. Slide the dowel through and your wall hanging is ready to display!

QAYG Table Runner

Materials:

- Fabric scraps or fat quarters for the top
- Batting (cut to 16" x 40" or desired table runner size)
- Backing fabric (cut to match the size of the batting)
- Thread
- Sewing machine

Steps:

Prepare Your Fabric: Cut your fabric scraps into strips or squares (about 2" to 6"). Consider using a combination of colors and patterns for visual interest.

Layer Batting and Backing: Cut the batting to your desired table runner size (16" x 40"). Place the batting on a flat surface and lay the backing fabric on top, wrong side facing down.

Arrange Fabric Pieces: Lay out your fabric strips or squares on top of the batting in a design you like. You can create a pattern or go for a more random arrangement.

Attach the First Piece: Place the first fabric piece right-side-up at one edge of the batting. Pin it in place.

Sew the Next Piece: Place the second piece right-side-down on top of the first piece, aligning the edges. Sew a ¼" seam along the edge where they meet.

Flip and Press: Flip the second piece right-side-up and press it flat with an iron. Continue adding fabric pieces until the entire batting area is covered, trimming any excess fabric as necessary.

Quilt the Runner: Optionally, sew along the seams or create additional quilting lines for texture.

Prepare the Backing: Cut a piece of backing fabric to match the size of the quilted top. Layer it on top of the quilted piece, right sides together. Sew around the edges, leaving an opening for turning.

Turn and Finish: Turn the table runner right-side-out through the opening. Press flat and topstitch around the edges to close the opening.

Add Final Touches: Consider adding a decorative stitch or quilting design on the surface of the table runner for extra flair.

QAYG Cozy Quilt

Materials:

- Fabric scraps in various colors and patterns (for a cozy look)
- Batting (cut to desired size, e.g., 60" x 72" for a lap quilt)
- Backing fabric (cut to match the size of the batting)
- Thread
- Sewing machine

Steps:

Prepare Your Fabric: Cut your fabric scraps into squares or rectangles (4" to 8"). Aim for a mix of colors and patterns to create a cozy patchwork effect.

Layer Batting and Backing: Cut the batting to the size of your quilt (60" x 72"). Layer it on a flat surface and place the backing fabric on top, wrong side facing down.

Design the Quilt Layout: Arrange your fabric squares or rectangles on top of the batting in your desired pattern.

Attach the First Piece: Place the first piece right-side-up at one corner of the batting.

Sew the Next Piece: Place the next piece right-side-down on top of the first piece, aligning the edges. Sew a ¼" seam along the edge where they meet.

Flip and Press: Flip the second piece right-side-up and press it with an iron. Continue adding pieces until the batting is fully covered.

Quilt the Cozy Quilt: Sew along the seams or create additional quilting lines for added texture and coziness.

Finish with Backing: Cut a backing fabric piece to match the size of the quilt top. Layer it on top of the quilted top, right sides together. Sew around the edges, leaving an opening for turning.

Turn and Finish: Turn the quilt right-side-out through the opening. Press it flat, and topstitch around the edges to close the opening.

Optional Binding: For a more finished look, consider adding binding around the edges of the quilt.

CHAPTER EIGHT
Advanced Qayg Projects

QAYG Bed Quilt

Materials:

- A variety of fabric scraps or fat quarters (consider using a color palette that coordinates well)
- Batting (cut into blocks, e.g., 12" x 12" or 10" x 10")
- Backing fabric (cut to match the size of the quilt)
- Thread
- Sewing machine
- Binding fabric

Steps:

Prepare Your Fabric: Cut your fabric scraps into squares or rectangles (10" to 12"). Aim for a mix of colors and patterns to create a visually striking design.

Cut the Batting: Cut the batting into blocks that match the size of your fabric squares (10" x 10" or 12" x 12"). You will need enough blocks to create the entire quilt.

Assemble the QAYG Blocks: Layer each batting square with fabric squares on top. Start with one fabric square, place it right-side-up on the batting. Add a second fabric square right-side-down on top of the first, aligning the edges. Sew a ¼" seam along one edge, flip it, and press.

Complete the QAYG Blocks: Continue adding fabric squares to each block until the batting is covered. You can create unique patterns for each block, such as log cabin or patchwork designs.

Quilt the Blocks: Quilt each block as desired, adding texture and interest. You can quilt straight lines, curves, or free-motion designs.

Assemble the Quilt Top: Once all blocks are complete, arrange them in the desired layout. Sew the blocks together using a ¼" seam allowance, matching seams as you go.

Add Backing and Binding: Cut the backing fabric to match the finished quilt top size. Layer it on top of the quilted blocks, right sides together, and sew around the edges, leaving an opening for turning. Turn the quilt right-side-out, press, and topstitch to close the opening. Attach the binding to finish the edges.

QAYG Memory Quilt

Materials:

- Fabric scraps (consider incorporating meaningful fabrics, such as clothing or fabric from special events)
- Batting (cut to desired size, e.g., 60" x 72")
- Backing fabric (cut to match the size of the quilt)
- Thread
- Sewing machine
- Decorative stitching materials (optional, such as embroidery thread or embellishments)

Steps:

Gather Your Fabrics: Collect fabric scraps that have sentimental value (like old shirts, baby clothes, or fabric from meaningful events). Cut them into various shapes (squares, rectangles, or other shapes) to create a unique layout.

Cut the Batting: Cut the batting to the size of your desired memory quilt (60" x 72").

Layer and Design Your Blocks: Lay out your fabric pieces on top of the batting, experimenting with different layouts to showcase your favorite fabrics. Aim for a balanced design that tells a story.

Assemble the QAYG Blocks: Start by placing the first fabric piece right-side-up on the batting. Pin it in place. Add a second piece right-side-down on top of the first, aligning the edges. Sew a ¼" seam along the edge, flip, and press.

Continue Adding Pieces: Continue this process with additional fabric pieces until each batting block is fully covered, ensuring that the design flows well throughout the quilt.

Quilt the Memory Quilt: Once all blocks are complete, consider adding personal touches like decorative stitching or embroidery on top of the fabric pieces to enhance the memory theme.

Sew the Blocks Together: Arrange the completed blocks in your desired layout and sew them together, ensuring to match seams carefully.

Prepare the Backing and Binding: Cut the backing fabric to match the size of the quilt. Layer it on top of the quilted top, right sides together. Sew around the edges, leaving an opening for turning. Turn right-side-out, press, and topstitch to close the opening. Attach the binding to finish the edges.

QAYG Starburst Quilt

Materials:

- Fabric in a range of colors (solids or prints)
- Batting (cut into blocks, e.g., 12" x 12" or 14" x 14")
- Backing fabric (cut to match the size of the quilt)
- Thread
- Sewing machine
- Binding fabric

Steps:

Prepare Your Fabrics: Select fabrics in colors that create a bold contrast for the starburst design. Cut the fabric into strips (2" to 6" wide) to create the starburst effect.

Cut Batting Squares: Cut batting into blocks of 12" or 14" depending on the size of the quilt. The starburst design will be created within each of these blocks.

Start the Starburst Design: Begin by placing the first fabric strip diagonally across the center of the batting block, right-side-up. Pin in place.

Add Strips to Form the Starburst: Lay the next fabric strip right-side-down, aligned with the edge of the first strip. Sew a ¼" seam along the edge, then flip the second strip right-side-up and press. Continue adding strips on both sides of the original strip, working outward until the batting is covered.

Quilt Each Block: Quilt along the seams or create additional quilting lines radiating out from the center for texture.

Join the Blocks: Once all blocks are complete, arrange them in a layout where the starburst designs align. Sew the blocks together, ensuring seams match.

Finish with Backing and Binding: Cut the backing fabric to match the size of the quilt top. Place the backing fabric right-side-down on top of the quilted blocks. Sew around the edges, leaving an opening to turn the quilt right-side-out. After turning, topstitch to close the opening. Add binding to finish the edges.

QAYG Hexagon Quilt

Materials:

- Fabric scraps or fat quarters in various colors and patterns

- Batting (cut into hexagonal shapes)
- Backing fabric
- Thread
- Sewing machine
- Hexagon templates
- Binding fabric

Steps:

Cut the Fabric and Batting: Use a hexagon template (6" or 8" sides) to cut hexagons out of both fabric and batting. You will need enough hexagons to complete the size of quilt you want.

Layer the Batting and Fabric: For each hexagon, place one fabric hexagon right-side-up on top of a batting hexagon.

Prepare the QAYG Hexagons: Use a smaller fabric hexagon (about 1" smaller than the batting) and place it on top of the larger fabric hexagon. Sew around the edges to secure the two layers of fabric and the batting together. Continue layering fabric and batting for each hexagon.

Quilt Each Hexagon: Quilt within each hexagon by stitching a spiral, straight lines, or other geometric patterns. This creates a strong texture and visual interest within each hexagonal block.

Join the Hexagons: Once all the hexagons are quilted, lay them out in your desired pattern. Sew the hexagons together using a Y-seam technique to create a seamless look.

Finish with Backing and Binding: Cut a backing fabric to match the size of the quilt. Place the backing fabric right-side-down, and sew around the edges, leaving a small opening. After turning the quilt right-side-out, close the opening with topstitching. Bind the edges using fabric strips cut on the bias to smoothly follow the hexagonal shapes.

QAYG Cathedral Window Quilt

Materials:

- Solid-colored fabric (for the frames)
- Printed fabric (for the "window" pieces)
- Batting (optional, depending on desired thickness)
- Thread
- Sewing machine
- Binding fabric

Steps:

Prepare the Fabric for Frames: Cut large squares from your solid fabric (e.g., 10" x 10"). These will form the base of each block, acting as the window "frames."

Create Folded Frames: Fold each square in half diagonally, wrong sides together, and press. Fold it again to create a smaller triangle. This folding method will form the curves of the cathedral windows later.

Prepare the Window Fabric: Cut smaller squares (e.g., 5" x 5") from your printed fabric. These will act as the "windows" in the quilt. Place a printed square on top of the base block's center.

Sew the Frame and Window Together: Unfold the base block, and with the window fabric square in place, fold the edges of the frame around it. Sew along the folded edges of the frame to secure the window fabric.

Quilt the Blocks: Quilt around the edges of the windows or add decorative stitching within the window space.

Assemble the Quilt Top: Arrange the quilt blocks in a pleasing layout, ensuring the window designs flow well together. Sew the blocks together using a ¼" seam allowance.

Add Backing and Binding: Cut the backing fabric to match the finished size of the quilt top. Layer the backing, and if desired, add batting between the quilt top and backing. Sew around the edges, leaving an opening for turning. Finish with binding to give the quilt a polished look.

QAYG Curved Piecing Quilt

Materials:

- A variety of fabric scraps (preferably solids and prints with high contrast)
- Batting (cut into blocks, e.g., 12" x 12")
- Backing fabric (cut to match the size of the quilt)
- Thread
- Curved piecing template or freehand cutting
- Sewing machine
- Binding fabric

Steps:

Cut Fabric for Curved Pieces: Use a curved piecing template (or freehand cut) to create curved pieces from your fabric scraps. You can make them half-circle, wavy, or irregular shapes to add complexity to your design.

Cut the Batting: Cut the batting into squares matching the size of the curved pieced blocks you plan to make (e.g., 12" x 12").

Begin Piecing Curves: Starting with one piece of fabric, place it right-side-up on the batting. Add the next piece of fabric, right-side-down, aligning the curved edges. Sew the two curved pieces together, following the curve carefully.

Add More Curved Pieces: Continue adding curved fabric pieces until the entire batting block is covered. Each curved seam should fit smoothly together without puckering, requiring careful sewing.

Quilt Each Block: Once the blocks are pieced together, quilt over the curved seams to add definition and texture. You can quilt lines that follow the natural curves or add free-motion quilting for additional interest.

Join the Blocks: Arrange the curved blocks in a cohesive layout and sew them together. Match the curves from block to block to create a flowing, dynamic quilt top.

Finish with Backing and Binding: Cut the backing fabric to the size of the quilt. Layer the quilt top, batting, and backing fabric. Sew around the edges, leaving an opening for turning. After turning the quilt right-side-out, close the opening with topstitching. Finish with binding to complete the quilt.

CHAPTER NINE
Troubleshooting and Tips

Troubleshooting Common Quilt as You Go (QAYG) Issues

Even experienced quilters may run into problems when working on Quilt as You Go (QAYG) projects.

Uneven Seams When Joining Blocks

Issue: Seams don't align or are bunched up when joining pre-quilted blocks.

Solution: Double-check your seam allowances. Ensure that the batting is trimmed slightly smaller than the fabric to avoid extra bulk at the seams. Use pins or clips to keep blocks perfectly aligned before sewing them together.

Quilt Blocks Shift During Quilting

Issue: Blocks move or shift while quilting, causing wrinkles or misaligned designs.

Solution: Secure each layer with spray adhesive or safety pins before quilting. This will hold the fabric in place, reducing movement. If using a sewing machine, guide the fabric gently without pulling it too hard.

Thread Tension Problems

Issue: The thread tension is uneven, leading to loose or tight stitches.

Solution: Adjust your sewing machine's tension settings based on the thickness of your quilt sandwich (fabric, batting, and backing). Test on a scrap piece of fabric with similar layers before quilting. For hand quilting, ensure your stitches are evenly spaced and not too tight to avoid puckering.

Fabric Puckering

Issue: The fabric puckers when quilting the layers together.

Solution: Make sure the fabric layers are smoothed out before quilting. Use a walking foot on your sewing machine to evenly feed the fabric layers through. Press the fabric blocks well before and after piecing to eliminate creases that may cause puckering.

Bulky Seams

Issue: Seams feel bulky where the batting overlaps between blocks.

Solution: Trim the batting within each block ¼" to ½" smaller than the fabric. This ensures that when joining blocks, the batting doesn't overlap excessively, reducing bulk. Also, press seams open or to one side, depending on which technique feels smoother.

Inconsistent Block Sizes

Issue: Blocks are different sizes, making it difficult to join them evenly.

Solution: Measure and cut each block with precision before quilting. Ensure consistent seam allowances when piecing the blocks. If a block turns out too small, consider adding a border around it to make it the correct size.

Difficulty Quilting Through Multiple Layers

Issue: Quilting through the quilt sandwich (top, batting, backing) is challenging due to the thickness.

Solution: Use a walking foot or free-motion foot for better control when quilting through thicker layers. Adjust your needle to a heavier gauge (e.g., 90/14) to handle thicker fabrics. For dense quilting patterns, reduce the stitch length slightly for smoother movement through the layers.

Fraying Fabric Edges

Issue: Fabric edges fray before the blocks are joined together.

Solution: Consider using pinking shears to cut fabric edges, which minimizes fraying. Alternatively, use a zigzag stitch or overlock stitch around the block edges before quilting to secure the fabric and prevent fraying.

Backing Fabric Shifts or Bunches

Issue: The backing fabric shifts or bunches during the final assembly.

Solution: Smooth the backing fabric on a flat surface before laying the quilted blocks on top. Use pins or spray adhesive to hold the backing in place while sewing. When quilting, start from the center and work outward to minimize fabric shifting.

Uneven Quilting Stitch Length

Issue: Quilting stitches vary in length or appear uneven.

Solution: If using a sewing machine, set the stitch length appropriately (typically longer for quilting, around 3.0). Practice guiding the fabric smoothly under the needle. For hand quilting, use a thimble to maintain consistent pressure, and work slowly to ensure evenly spaced stitches.

Mismatched Binding

Issue: The binding does not fit or align properly with the edges of the quilt.

Solution: Measure and cut binding strips carefully, ensuring they are long enough to fit all around the quilt. When attaching the binding, use clips or pins to secure it evenly before sewing. Mitre the corners for a neat finish, and trim any excess fabric from the edges to avoid mismatches.

General Tips for Quilt as You Go (QAYG)

Quilt as You Go (QAYG) offers a unique, block-by-block approach to quilting, making it easier to handle large projects and achieve precise results. Below are some general tips to ensure a smooth and successful quilting experience.

Start with Simple Designs: For beginners, it's helpful to start with simple blocks and patterns to get a feel for the QAYG process. Straight-line piecing or simple geometric designs are easier to manage when working with individual blocks.

Accurate Measurements are Key: Always measure and cut your fabric and batting accurately. Use a rotary cutter, ruler, and cutting mat to ensure straight, clean cuts. Consistency in block sizes helps when joining blocks together, leading to a more professional finish.

Use the Right Needle and Thread: Choose a needle appropriate for the thickness of your layers. A quilting needle or a heavy-duty needle (e.g., size 90/14) works well for sewing through multiple layers. Opt for high-quality cotton or polyester thread to withstand the rigors of quilting.

Press Seams for Accuracy: Pressing seams between steps is critical to achieving flat, even blocks. Pressing seams open or to one side helps prevent bulk, especially where blocks are joined. Always press your blocks after sewing to keep them neat.

Stay Organized: Label your blocks, especially for larger projects, so you can easily track their placement and orientation. This helps ensure that when you assemble the quilt, everything is in the correct order and design.

Test Your Stitch Settings: Before quilting the actual blocks, test your sewing machine's stitch length and tension on a scrap piece of fabric with similar layers. For hand quilting, practice even stitches on a smaller piece before starting the full project.

Use a Walking Foot for Even Quilting: A walking foot is a must-have for QAYG, especially when quilting through multiple layers. It helps feed the fabric evenly, preventing puckering or distortion in the quilt sandwich.

Trim Batting for Seam Allowances: When quilting individual blocks, trim the batting slightly smaller than the fabric pieces. This prevents the batting from overlapping at the seams when joining blocks, reducing bulk and creating smoother joins.

Experiment with Quilt Designs: QAYG allows for creative freedom with your quilt top. Since you're working block by block, you can experiment with different quilting patterns and designs for each block. Mix straight-line quilting with free-motion or hand quilting for a unique look.

Secure Your Layers: To prevent shifting while quilting, use basting spray, pins, or safety pins to secure the fabric, batting, and backing layers. This step ensures that all the layers stay aligned and reduces the risk of wrinkles during quilting.

Quilt from the Center Out: When quilting each block, start from the center and work outward. This helps distribute the fabric evenly and minimizes puckering or bunching. If you quilt from one side to the other, the fabric might shift or gather in one area.

Plan Your Layout in Advance: Before joining your blocks, lay them out to decide on the final arrangement. This is especially important if you're working with different fabric patterns or colors. Rearranging blocks beforehand allows you to create a cohesive design.

Take Your Time: QAYG can be more time-consuming than traditional quilting methods since you're quilting each block individually. However, taking your time to piece, press, and quilt each block ensures a higher-quality final result.

Choose the Right Batting: Depending on the look and feel you want, choose batting with the right thickness and loft. Cotton batting works well for traditional quilts, while polyester batting gives a fluffier finish. Make sure your batting is cut evenly for each block.

Finish with Binding: Once you've joined all the blocks, bind your quilt carefully. Cut your binding strips evenly and sew them with care to avoid puckering. For neat, professional-looking corners, try a mitred binding finish.

Incorporate Decorative Elements: Don't be afraid to add embellishments such as appliqué, embroidery, or decorative stitching to individual blocks. Since QAYG is done in smaller sections, adding these elements is easier than doing them on a full-sized quilt.

CONCLUSION

Quilt as You Go (QAYG) is a versatile and beginner-friendly technique that allows quilters to tackle even large projects one block at a time. By following the step-by-step methods outlined in this guide, you can master both basic and advanced QAYG techniques, develop a strong understanding of fabric selection, and create cohesive designs. From choosing the right tools and fabrics to troubleshooting common issues, this approach not only simplifies quilting but also opens up opportunities for creativity and customization.

As you grow more comfortable with QAYG, you'll discover the freedom and flexibility it offers, allowing you to experiment with different patterns, quilting methods, and even embellishments. Whether you're quilting by hand or machine, the QAYG technique ensures that your projects are more manageable, making quilting enjoyable and less overwhelming. With practice and patience, you'll be able to create stunning, professional-quality quilts with a personal touch.

Printed in Dunstable, United Kingdom